mybook 2

Off the RECORD

SCHOLASTIC INC.

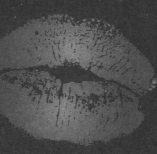

Photos ©: Dreamstime: Creativei, Monykwe; iStockphoto: A-Digit, Diane Labombarbe, doodlemachine, GeorgePeters, highhorse, kanyakits, Michelle Schiro, NejroN, Shunrei, shuoshu, TracyBarbas, trinitic, Yakovliev; Shutterstock, Inc.: Aleks Melnik, Aleynikov Pavel, AnastasiaSonne, Andrey_Kuzmin, Andriy Zholudyev, Anna Kutukova, Anna Paff, Annykos, ARENA Creative, artshock, Axro, Ben Branham, best works, bioraven, Boris Zatserkovnyy, Bukhavets Mikhail, CataVic, cepera, chronicler, chyworks, Cvijun, Dahabian, Digiselector, Dimec, Doremi, Dr_Flash, dumbgrep, Elena Medvedeva, Faberr Ink, florik, Good Vector, Gorbash Varvara, grmarc, grop, gubgib, gudinny, Hopeful.ya, Incomible, Inna Ogando, Irina Kouznetsova, isaxar, Jiri Vaclavek, Julia Tim, jumpingsack, Just Keep Drawing, karen roach, KennyK, kokitom, kontur-vid, Kseniia Romanova, kstudija, Ladoga, Lavandaart, lekalovich, Les Perysty, Leszek Glasner, LHF Graphics, lineartestpilot, Little Sparrow, Lorelinka, Lorelyn Medina, Maaike Boot, Macrovector, Magnia, makar, MaKars, MargaritaS, Marie Nimrichterova, MD tat, Minii Ho, mixform design, MyClipArtStore.com, Natalia Hubbert, Natalia Semenchenko, Natalyon, Oleksiy Mark, Olga Lobareva, Olga_Angelloz, Olga1818, pashabo, Pelonmaker, Picsfive, Pushistaja, R_lion_O, R. Formidable, redchocolate, Regine, Ron and Joe, Roomline, Ruslan Kokarev, Sanotina, Seamartini Graphics, Serg Shalimoff, Sonya illustration, Sooa, tapilipa, Tatiana Akhmetgalieva, terwijl, TheBlackRhino, Transfuchsian, Tribalium, Tropinina Olga, tsaplia, Vidux, Vladgrin, Vook, wallnarez, xpixel, Yulia Glam, Yulia Yemelianova, yusuf doganay, zayats-and-zayats, Zlatko Guzmic; Thinkstock: Lisa F. Young, owattaphotos.

ISBN 978-0-545-84897-8

10 9 8 7 6 5 4 3 2 1   15 16 17 18 19/0

Printed in China 95
First printing 2015

Written by **ELIZABETH SCHAEFER**
Art Direction by **PAUL W. BANKS**
Designed by **ROCCO MELILLO**

ABOUT THIS BOOK:

THERE'S ONE THING THAT YOU ARE THE WORLD'S BIGGEST EXPERT ON—YOU! THIS BOOK IS PACKED FULL OF QUIZZES, ACTIVITIES, AND OTHER FUN QUESTIONS THAT ONLY YOU CAN ANSWER. READY? THEN TURN THE PAGE AND GET STARTED!

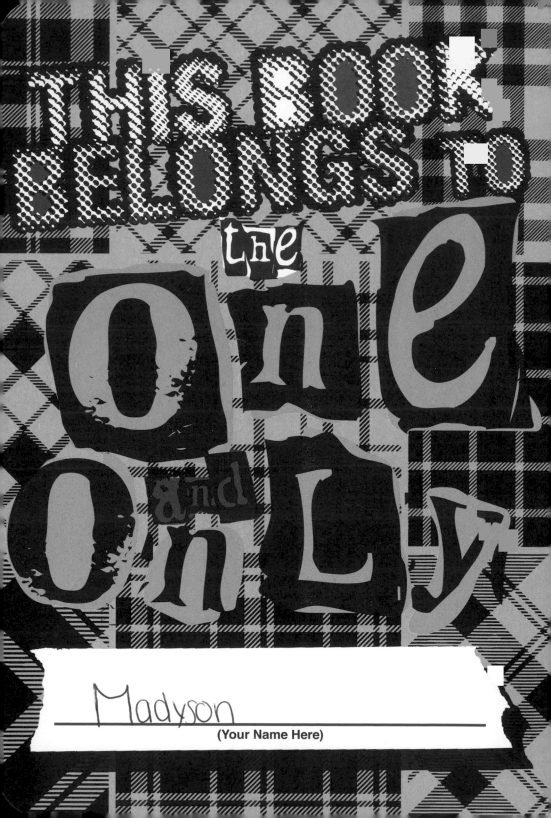

THIS BOOK BELONGS TO

the One and Only

Madyson

(Your Name Here)

#MYSELFIE

THE Map to My

to My

MOM

CRUSH

ME MOM

With parents, siblings, BFFs, frenemies, and crushes, your world can get a little cray! Sort it all out with a guide to all the weird and wild connections that make up your life. There are a few circles here to get you started. Just add in names and draw a picture of that person. Then draw new circles to add everyone else in your world — pets, teachers, whoever you want!

The ABC'S

A Accessory you can't live without:

B Biggest pet peeve:

C Can't stand:

D Dream car:

E Everyone deserves:

F First thing people notice about you:

G Geeky obsession:

H Hairstyle:

I Inside joke:

J Just watched:

K Kilts: Hot or not?

L Last movie you saw:

M Middle name:

8

# of ME

N Number of friends online: ☐

O Oldest friend: ☐

P Perfect date: ☐

Q Quit this bad habit: ☐

R Real friends always: ☐

S Secret crush: ☐

T Top talent: ☐

U Umbrellas or raincoats? ☐

V Very first memory: ☐

W Worst mistake: ☐

X Xciting news: ☐

Y You can always trust: ☐

Z Zip it! What's your biggest secret?

☐

my faves

I looove this stuff!

Movie _D.U.F.F_

TV show _____

Food _____

Animal _____

Celebrity _____

Online video _____

Book _____

Style of shoe _____

Class at school _____

Color of nail polish _____

Country _____

Fictional character _____

Scent _____

Dance move _____

Store _____

Sport _____

Boy's name _____

Girl's name _____

Hashtag _____

Candy _____

Song _____

Video game _____

Soda _____

App _____

Place to hang _____

Cartoon _____

my not-so faves

KILL IT WITH FIRE!

Movie _____

TV show _____

Food _____

Animal _____

Celebrity _____

Online video _____

Book _____

Style of shoe _____

Class at school _____

Color of nail polish _____

Country _____

Fictional character _____

Scent _____

Dance move _____

Store _____

Sport _____

Boy's name _____

Girl's name _____

Hashtag _____

Candy _____

Song _____

Video game _____

Soda _____

App _____

Place to hang _____

Cartoon _____

WHAT MESSAGE WOULD YOU LIKE TO FIND IN A FORTUNE COOKIE?

Write your own fortunes about your school, your crush, and your future:

SCHOOL:

CRUSH:

FUTURE:

Make a list of everything inside your backpack and purse.

Circle the most important things.
Cross out everything you'd rather ditch!

_____   _____   _____

_____   _____   _____

_____   _____   _____

_____   _____   _____

_____   _____   _____

_____   _____   _____

14

ARE YOU A Country Girl OR A City Girl?

You can't live without:

A. Your pet
B. Your phone
C. Sunshine
D. Coffee

Your perfect Saturday would be:

A. Waking up early and checking out some hiking trails
B. Hanging out with your friends at the new coffee shop
C. Sitting outside to read your fave book
D. Going to the movies to see the latest blockbuster

Which of these outfits sounds like you?

A. A comfy sweater, jeans, and sneakers
B. A polka-dot miniskirt with a button-down blouse and matching high heels
C. A flowy skirt with an organic cotton tank top
D. A chevron print dress inspired by your fave fashion blog

Your dream home is:

A. A simple cottage with a garden
B. A trendy new apartment
C. A farm filled with animals
D. A mansion with tons of space

Results

Mostly A's and C's:

Yeehaw! You're a country girl, through and through. Totes in sync with nature, your simple style and down-to-earth attitude are a breath of fresh air!

Mostly B's and D's:

It's bright lights, big city for you! You're a city girl who totes loves the noise and energy of places like New York and LA. Whether it's a big day of shopping or an evening at the movies, the city is the place for all the things you love.

DING, DONG!

Someone just left a giant package for you on your doorstep. What's inside?! Draw it here:

There's a 1ST time for EVERYTHING!

> **FIRST MOVIE YOU SAW IN A MOVIE THEATER:**

polar express

> **FIRST PERSON YOU HAD A CRUSH ON:**

> **FIRST GRADE TEACHER:** Ms. Davis

> **FIRST PERSON YOU TEXTED TODAY:** No one

> **FIRST CONCERT YOU WENT TO:** NONE

> **FIRST STATE YOU LIVED IN:** Maryland

EVEN THE BEST GET
STRESSED!

Make a list of all the things that make you feel totally **wiped**. Then cross each stressful thing out and write down something next to it that helps you **chillax** instead.

HASHTAGS

WRITE IN YOUR OWN STATUSES
TO MATCH THESE HASHTAGS.

#sorryimnotsorry

#bestdayever

#FTW!
(for the win!)

_____
_____
_____
_____
_____

_____ **#justsaying**

_____
_____
_____
_____

_____ **#livingthedream**

_____
_____
_____
_____

_____ **#noregrets**

DREAM BIG

Imagine your fab future life...

5 years from now:

You live in

You've traveled to

You have a pet

You go to school at

You're best friends with

10 years from now:

You live in

You have your dream job as a

You've become the first person to ever

You've invented a new

Your fave place to go on vacay is

#MYFLAIR

WATCH OUT WORLD

Nothing can stop you when you're rocking a can-do up-do or some hard-core highlights. Draw your fiercest hairstyle statement here:

How well do you know your BFF's

Grab your BFF and get ready for a closet quiz! Use the questions below to see how much she knows about your fashion faves.

MUST-HAVE ACCESSORY?

FASHION ICON?

SHOES?

COLOR?

HAIRSTYLE?

LIP GLOSS FLAVOR?

NAIL POLISH?

SKINNY JEANS   OR   BOOT CUT?

JEWELRY: GOLD   OR   SILVER?

FASHION PET PEEVE?

Now flip the page and pass this book to your BFF. Have her quiz you to see how much you really know about her!

How well do you know your BFF's

Grab your BFF and get ready for a closet quiz!
Use the questions below to see how much she
knows about your fashion faves.

MUST-HAVE ACCESSORY?

FASHION ICON?

SHOES?

COLOR?

HAIRSTYLE?

LIP GLOSS FLAVOR?

NAIL POLISH?

SKINNY JEANS   OR   BOOT CUT?

JEWELRY: GOLD   OR   SILVER?

FASHION PET PEEVE?

SSShhhh!

Write down some of your best-kept fashion secrets...

An accessory that can make any outfit is

I love to pair my skinny jeans with

My never-fail nail polish is

A totes amaze hair product is

My go-to shoes are

Rock THE RUNWAY!

List the top five songs you'd play as you strut your style on the catwalk.

1. _____

2. _____

3. _____

4. _____

5. _____

Extreme Room MAKEOVER

What if you could completely redesign your room?
What would you change? What would you want to keep exactly the same?
Imagine everything about your totally tricked-out pad here:

You have a **FLAIR FOR FASHION** that's all your own. But what is the perfect style when it comes to your **CRUSH?**

Your dream guy is always walking around in:

A. Classic black Converse

B. Sleek sneakers

C. Dressy leather lace-ups

D. Comfy flip-flops

To keep track of the time, your crush uses:

A. A pocket watch

B. A waterproof wrist watch

C. A Rolex

D. His phone. Who wants to carry an extra accessory?

Time for prom! Your date pairs his suit with:

A. A plaid bowtie

B. A clip-on tie

C. A tie that perfectly matches your dress

D. No tie at all—they're way too itchy

When it comes to hot hairstyles, your perfect guy has:

A. A close cut on the sides with a punk sweep on top

B. A buzz cut

C. Any length hair, but it's styled to perfection

D. The "Just rolled out of bed" look

Mostly A's:

Your perfect guy puts the "hip" in hipster. Just make sure he doesn't steal your skinny jeans!

Mostly B's:

Your sporty crush's simple style means he's always ready for action. But he probably won't be running to a designer outlet any time soon!

Results

Mostly C's:

In any sitch, your dream guy is ready to show off his swanky style. Classy is always in fashion!

Mostly D's:

Your perfect date isn't exactly a trendsetter. But being comfortable with who you are can be the ultimate accessory!

POW!

When fashion disasters strike, you are there to save the day. Design your own superhero costume that shows off your signature style. Don't forget to create your own super symbol!

Freaky fashion Friday!

What if you could switch wardrobes with anyone in your class. Who would you switch with and why?

DRAW YOUR FASHION TRANSPLANT HERE:

YOU

WHO?

WHY?

34

My SWEET RIDE

When it comes to colors, you think:

A. Rich tones are ideal

B. Soft and natural is the way to go

C. The bolder the better

What kind of car fits your style?

Your fave place to shop is:

A. A designer boutique

B. A secondhand store

C. The mall

It's picture day! You make sure to wear:

A. A cashmere sweater

B. Your comfy khakis

C. Your biggest pair of hoop earrings

You wouldn't be caught dead wearing:

A. Ripped jeans

B. 5-inch heels

C. A drab brown skirt

Results

MOSTLY A's:

For you, a stretch limo is the only way to travel! You love luxe, and you're not afraid to show it.

MOSTLY B's:

A compact hybrid is more your style. Smooth and dependable, your car will really go the distance.

MOSTLY C's:

A flashy red sports car is just your speed. When you rev the engine, everyone turns to look — and that's just the way you like it.

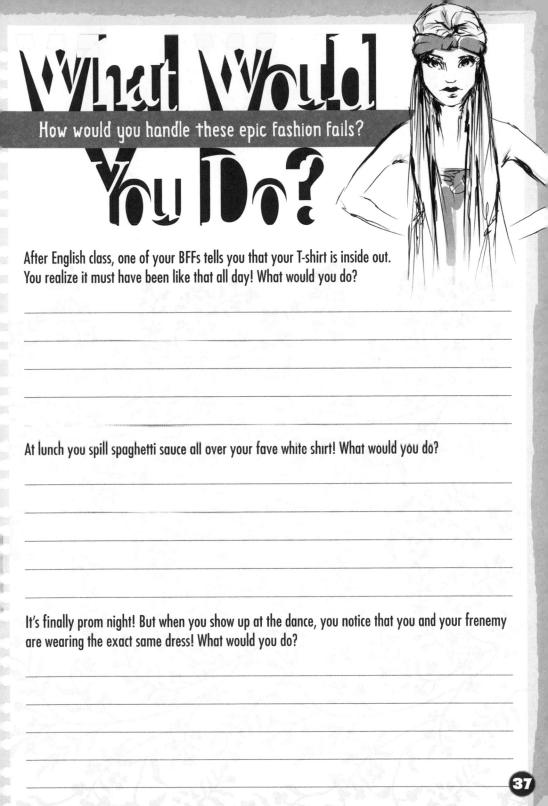

What Would

You Do?

After English class, one of your BFFs tells you that your T-shirt is inside out. You realize it must have been like that all day! What would you do?

_____

_____

_____

_____

At lunch you spill spaghetti sauce all over your fave white shirt! What would you do?

_____

_____

_____

_____

It's finally prom night! But when you show up at the dance, you notice that you and your frenemy are wearing the exact same dress! What would you do?

_____

_____

_____

_____

MyStyle, Inc.

If you were a fashion designer, you would

be famous for _____

Your HQ would be in _____

You'd even design clothes for celebrities

like _____

and _____!

Write about your first big fashion show here:

_____

_____

_____

_____

Design your own label here:

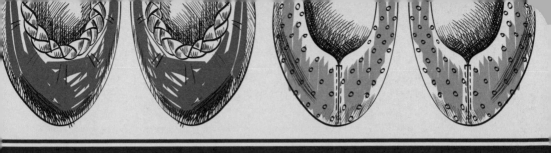

Shoe Scramble!

Without looking at your closet, describe every pair of shoes you own. <u>No peeking!</u>

_____   _____

_____   _____

_____   _____

_____   _____

_____   _____

_____   _____

Now, check this list against your shoe rack. <u>Did you forget any?</u>

WOULD YOU RATHER...

☑ CHECK THE BOX

☐ WEAR THE SAME SHIRT EVERY DAY FOR A YEAR **OR** ☐ NEVER BE ABLE TO WEAR THE SAME SHIRT TWICE?

☐ DRESS LIKE YOU'RE FROM THE 80S **OR** ☐ DRESS LIKE YOU'RE 8?

☐ HAVE TO SEW YOUR OWN CLOTHES **OR** ☐ WEAR HAND-ME-DOWNS FOREVER?

☐ WEAR WINTER BOOTS TO THE BEACH **OR** ☐ WEAR FLIP-FLOPS IN A SNOWSTORM?

☐ HAVE TAN LINES ON YOUR FACE **OR** ☐ HAVE AN ORANGEY SPRAY TAN?

☐ ONLY WEAR BLACK **OR** ☐ ONLY WEAR CAMOUFLAGE?

40

#MYFLIX

Queen *of the* Silver Screen

(circle one)

I like superhero movies   more / less   than rom coms.

I prefer to watch   one movie at a time / movie marathons

I usually watch movies   at home / at the movie theater

I'd rather see a movie with   my friends / a date

At the movie theater, I love to get   popcorn / candy

3-D movies are   totes amaze / overrated

The perfect time to catch the latest blockbuster is   an afternoon matinee / a midnight showing

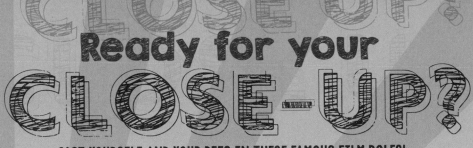

Ready for your CLOSE-UP?

CAST YOURSELF AND YOUR BFFS IN THESE FAMOUS FILM ROLES!

Katniss Everdeen _____
FROM *THE HUNGER GAMES*

Dorothy _____
FROM *THE WIZARD OF OZ*

Elizabeth Bennet _____
FROM *PRIDE AND PREJUDICE*

Hermione Granger _____
FROM *HARRY POTTER*

Queen Elsa _____
FROM *FROZEN*

AND THE **AWARD** GOES TO...

BEST

MOVIE TO WATCH WHEN YOU'RE SICK

_____

TEARJERKER

_____

MOVIE TO QUOTE

_____

MOVIE TO CHEER YOU UP

_____

MOVIE FOR A SLUMBER PARTY

_____

SCI-FI MOVIE

_____

ACTION MOVIE

_____

DATE MOVIE

_____

MOVIE OF ALL TIME

_____

QUOTE-A-PALOOZA!

Write down all your fave movie quotes here:

movie: _____

quote: _____

_____

movie: _____

quote: _____

_____

movie: _____

quote: _____

_____

movie: _____

quote: _____

_____

From Page to
Screen

List your five fave books that you wish someone would make a movie of! Then cast your fave stars as the leads.

Book: _____

*Star: _____

Book: _____

*Star: _____

Book: _____

*Star: _____

Book: _____

*Star: _____

Book: _____

*Star: _____

WHAT KIND OF MOVIE ST★R ARE YOU?

In your latest film, you play:

- A. A glam socialite from the 1940s
- B. A scientist fighting against a mega corporation
- C. A snarky rock star

When you're not filming, you're:

- A. Researching your next role
- B. Campaigning for causes that are important to you
- C. Hitting all the biggest Hollywood parties

On the red carpet, you wear:

- A. A fit-and-flair evening gown
- B. A wrap dress made with organic fabrics
- C. A neon sheath dress with your fave 6-inch heels

Big news! You're going to be on the cover of:

- A. Vogue
- B. TIME
- C. People

Mostly A's:

Mostly B's:

Mostly C's:

HOLLYWOOD

Results

Hollywood Royalty

Your iconic glitz and glam make you the envy of everyone.

Activist Actor

You use your fame to make the world a better place.

Daring Diva

You make your own rules — everyone else needs to keep up!

SOUNDTRACK
TO YOUR LIFE!

If your life were a movie, write down
the songs that would play:

WHEN YOU WAKE UP:

AFTER YOU ACE A TEST:

**DURING AN ARGUMENT
WITH YOUR BESTIE:**

**ON THE LAST DAY OF
SCHOOL:**

**AFTER YOU SCORE THE
WINNING POINT:**

DURING MATH CLASS:

**WHEN YOUR CRUSH ASKS
YOU TO THE DANCE:**

Movie Quote MIX-UP

Circle one phrase in each numbered box:

1
FASHION SENSE
CUPCAKES
SEQUINS

2
THE FRIDGE
WISCONSIN
THE SPA

3
THAT'S GROSS
AWKWARD
PIZZA'S HERE

4
CAFETERIA
BROOM CLOSET
DANCE FLOOR

5
THE MALL
SUMMER CAMP
THE ICE CREAM TRUCK

Now, fill in the numbered blanks to create a hilarious new movie quote!

"WITH GREAT _____, COMES GREAT RESPONSIBILITY."
(1)

"THERE'S NO PLACE LIKE _____."
(2)

"LOVE MEANS NEVER HAVING TO SAY _____."
(3)

"I'M THE KING OF THE _____."
(4)

"TO INFINITY, AND _____."
(5)

make my movie!

Imagine you're pitching your next big movie to a studio. Describe the **CAN'T-MISS** story line below. Then, decide who will star in your **MEGA BLOCKBUSTER.**

STARRING

THIS **OR** THAT

CIRCLE ONE

Comedies **OR** Tearjerkers

Science fiction **OR** Horror movies

Live tweet **OR** Blog later

Indie movies **OR** Action blockbusters

Snarky commenting **OR** Silent movie-watching

Rewatch your faves **OR** Try something new

Witty one-liners **OR** Thought-provoking dialogue

52

So Bad IT'S GOOD!

We all have those movies that we totally love — but would never admit it!
List your top five guilty pleasure movies below:

1. _____

2. _____

3. _____

4. _____

5. _____

What was the name of the movie?

What made it so creeptastic?

You Oughta Be In Pictures!

If you were a character in a movie, what type of leading lady would you be?

Your character walks into a crowded store, when suddenly:

- A. You notice the manager is acting totes suspicious. Time to investigate!
- B. You bump into a cute guy and fall head over heels. Literally.
- C. You discover there's a bomb inside, and you have 90 seconds to turn it off

Your character's biggest challenge is:

- A. Finding a new clue
- B. Figuring out a hot guy's number
- C. Keeping nuclear launch codes safe from villains

Your character is most likely to go on a date with:

- A. The handsome cop who's helping you crack the case
- B. The journalist who's doing a story on your popular fashion bog
- C. A kick-butt secret agent

Right before the credits roll, your character is:

- A. Locking up the criminal you finally tracked down
- B. Walking into the sunset with the perfect guy
- C. Shaking hands with the president after saving her life

Results

Mostly A's:

It's elementary — you are the detective who can solve any case!

Mostly B's:

You are the quirky star of a rom com who's sure to find the man of her dreams.

Mostly C's:

Put on your sunglasses as you walk away from that explosion — you are an action star!

THE REEL YOU

Circle One!

True or *False*
If I'm bored during a movie, I'll fast forward through the slow parts.

True or *False*
Vampire movies are so over.

True or *False*
I own over 30 DVDs/Blu-rays.

True or *False*
The original is always better than the remake.

True or *False*
I hate movies that are really gory.

True or *False*
Movies have to be historically accurate or it drives me crazy.

True or *False*
I rewatch my fave scenes over and over.

True or *False*
Going to the movies is a perfect first date.

Coming Soon . . .

NERDTASTIC NUMBERS!

Fill in the blanks to share your tech talents.

> I SEND _____ TEXTS A DAY.

> I CAN TYPE _____ WORDS A MINUTE.

> I HAVE _____ FOLLOWERS.

> I'VE DOWNLOADED _____ APPS.

> I'M ONLINE ABOUT _____ MINUTES A DAY.

> MY HIGH SCORE IN MY FAVE GAME IS _____.

> I SUBSCRIBE TO _____ VIDEO CHANNELS.

WOULD YOU RATHER . . .

Circle one answer for each question.

Give up texting for a week
OR
Give up dessert for a month?

Travel to the future
OR
Travel to the past?

Have a home movie theater
OR
Have the world's fastest computer?

Have a phone from the 90s
OR
Have a TV from the 90s?

Lose all your phone contacts
OR
Lose your fave necklace?

Have a robot that
cleans your room
OR
Have a flying car?

BEST OF THE WEB

List your top five websites and what makes them so refreshable!

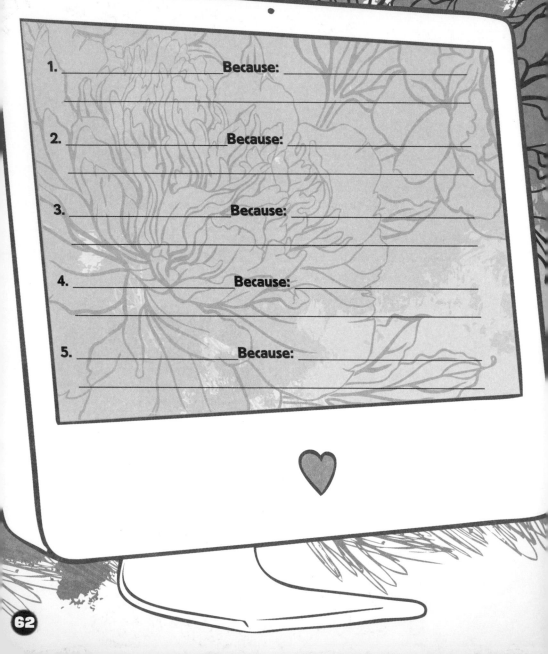

1. _____Because: _____

_____

2. _____Because: _____

_____

3. _____Because: _____

_____

4. _____Because: _____

_____

5. _____Because: _____

_____

HOW TECH SAVVY ARE YOU?

When you want to watch a movie you:

A. Stream something on your tablet

B. Grab a DVD from your bookshelf

C. Hook up your computer to play videos on your TV

D. Go out to the theater

You want to chat with your BFF. You:

A. Send her a text

B. Give her a call

C. Send her a DM

D. WrIte her a note

You and your besties have to do a group project for class. You:

A. Video chat and share files through your cloud drive

B. Meet at the library to do some research

C. Create a digital presentation with audio and video clips

D. Build a diorama

After you snap a pic, you:

A. Add your fave filter and post it online

B. Print out a copy and frame it

C. Add a hilar caption and text it to a friend

D. Save it on your phone and forget about it

social

Results

MOSTLY A'S AND C'S:

You are a tech maven! No matter how fast things change, you're always on top of every tech trend.

MOSTLY B'S AND D'S:

Tech isn't your priority. There's nothing wrong with handwriting a note to show you care.

See the World through Tech Glasses!

What if you had glasses that could instantly search the Internet for info about anything you looked at?

How would that change . . .

TAKING TESTS AT SCHOOL:

_____
_____
_____
_____

CHATTING WITH FRIENDS:

_____
_____
_____
_____

TRAVELING SOMEWHERE FOR THE FIRST TIME:

_____
_____
_____
_____

DOING CHORES:

_____
_____
_____
_____

Time MACHINE TROUBLES

Have you ever wished you could go back in time and undo a mistake? Write about your most epic fail here and what you would do to change it:

Top Tech
Tweets

Write in your own statuses to match these tech-tacular hashtags.

_____

_____

_____

_____#nextbigthing

_____

_____

_____

_____

_____#techoftomorrow

_____

_____

_____

_____#techproblems

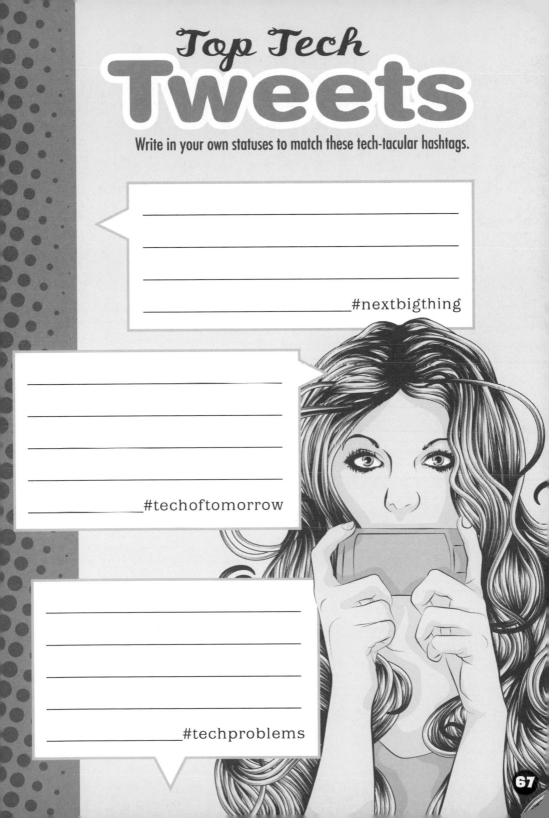

Invent a
MACHINE

that can do one of your lamest chores for you! Describe how your invention works here, then draw a picture.

DON'T FORGET TO GIVE IT A FAB NAME!

_____
_____
_____
_____
_____
_____
_____
_____

Draw it here:

Search

If you had your own online video channel, what would it be about? Would you sing covers of your top tunes? Or teach viewers all about your fave hobby? Or vlog about the juiciest celebrity gossip? Get creative and come up with your own unique feed!

Name your channel and design its logo below:

TOP VIDEO #1

TOP VIDEO #2

About my page:

_____

_____

_____

_____

_____

_____

What Would YOU Do?

Oh, no! You accidently spill soda all over your friend's brand-new phone. **What would you do?**

_____

_____

_____

_____

You're about to hand in that **big English paper.** But right before you pass it to your teacher, you notice a terrible typo on the first page. **What would you do?**

_____

_____

_____

_____

Your crush asks you to help him install a new program on his laptop. Of course you agree! The only problem? You have no idea how to actually do it! **What would you do?**

_____

_____

_____

_____

CRUNCH
the numbers

A = 3
B = 6
C = 9
D = 12
E = 15
F = 18
G = 21
H = 24
I = 1
J = 4
K = 7
L = 10
M = 13

N = 16
O = 19
P = 22
Q = 25
R = 2
S = 5
T = 8
U = 11
V = 14
W = 17
X = 20
Y = 23
Z = 26

Do you and your crush add up? Or are you destined for a long division? Write out your name and your crush's name below. Then use the letter/number chart to add up the letters in your names and get your compatibility number.

Add your love numbers together to get your compatibility score, then check the next page for your results!

YOUR CRUSH'S NAME

YOUR NAME

YOUR CRUSH'S LOVE NUMBER

YOUR LOVE NUMBER

Results

100+ Wow! Your compatibility is off the charts. Maybe it's time to work up your courage and tell him how you feel!

75–99 The love is strong with this one! You two probably have a lot in common. Try talking to him about one of your shared interests and see if sparks fly!

51–74 Things might be a little lukewarm, but don't give up! Every story has a beginning — who knows what might lead to your happily ever after.

26–50 There might not be an eternal flame here, but there's definitely a spark. Keep your friendship going and who knows what could happen!

1–25 He might not be the one for you. Get to know him better and find out for yourself!

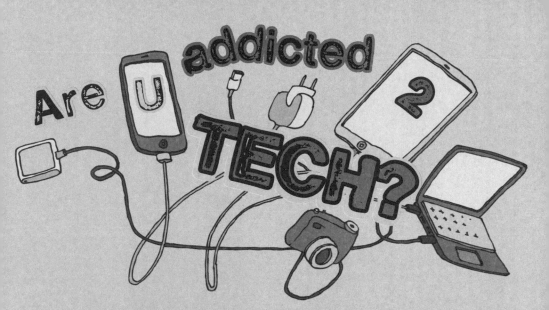

Are U addicted 2 TECH?

When you get home from school, the first thing you do is:

- A. Grab a snack
- B. Start your homework
- C. Stream some videos on your tablet
- D. Check your phone for texts

How much time do you spend online each day?

- A. 15 minutes
- B. Half an hour
- C. An hour
- D. Waaaay more than an hour

Time for a camping trip! You pack:

- A. Chocolate, marshmallows, and graham crackers. S'mores FTW!
- B. Your trusty pocketknife
- C. Your phone, your tablet, and your iPod
- D. Nothing. There's no way you'd go camping—no electricity!

The power goes out. What is your first thought?

- A. Better grab a flashlight
- B. Maybe school will be canceled!
- C. Ahhh! But I need my computer!
- D. At least my phone still has some battery left

Results

Mostly A's and B's:

Tech is crazy useful, but it doesn't run your life. There are plenty of other things to check out, too!

Mostly C's and D's:

OMG. You would DIE without your tech. Just remember to keep everything charged or you might have to go 15 minutes without your phone. *shudder*

Autocorrect x Fails

Sometimes autocorrect can be the worst! Suddenly your innocent text about your "dog" becomes "My dad is barking super loud tonight." Awkward! Write down your most embarrassing autocorrect fails here:

OMG!

What?!

???

are you GAME?

Design your own video game—
STARRING YOU!

🕹️ **MY VIDEO GAME IS CALLED** _____

🕹️ **THE HERO OF THE GAME IS** _____

🕹️ **TO WIN, THE PLAYER HAS TO** _____

🕹️ **BUT THERE ARE LOTS OF OBSTACLES!**

LIKE _____

AND _____

🕹️ **THE MAIN VILLAIN OF THE GAME IS** _____

🕹️ **IF IT'S EVER TOO HARD, THE PLAYER CAN GET HELP FROM**

_____

Imagine each level has its own location. List them here:

LEVEL 1: _____   LEVEL 4: _____

LEVEL 2: _____   LEVEL 5: _____

LEVEL 3: _____   LEVEL 6: _____

Plan a party to CELEBRATE YOUR BFFS!

First, pick a date that works for all your friends: _____

Where will you have the party? Pick somewhere that has a special meaning to you:

_____

Now decorate it with things that remind you of all your most hilar inside jokes. List them here: _____

_____

Pick some songs to play. What are your top friendship anthems?

_____

What kind of party games will you play? _____

_____

Looks like you've got it all planned out! Now you just have to let everyone know.

Draw an awesome invitation here:

YOUR ULTIMATE PARTY PLAYLIST!

List your top ten songs that are guaranteed to get a party bumpin'!

1. _____
2. _____
3. _____
4. _____
5. _____
6. _____
7. _____
8. _____
9. _____
10. _____

YOUR
PIC
HERE

National ME DAY

What if there were a national holiday all about you?

THE NAME OF YOUR HOLIDAY WOULD BE: _____

ON YOUR HOLIDAY, IT'S TRADITION FOR EVERYONE TO _____

_____

EVERYONE DECORATES FOR YOUR HOLIDAY WITH _____

_____

ON THE MORNING OF YOUR HOLIDAY, THE FIRST THING EVERYONE

DOES IS _____

THEN FOR LUNCH, EVERYONE ALWAYS EATS _____

_____

_____

NOW IT'S TIME FOR THE PARADE! DESCRIBE IT HERE: _____

_____

_____

_____

_____

IS THERE A NATIONAL SONG EVERYONE SINGS ON YOUR HOLIDAY?
WRITE OUT THE LYRICS HERE: _____

_____

_____

_____

_____

_____

ARE THERE ANY OTHER SPECIAL EVENTS THAT TAKE
PLACE ON YOUR HOLIDAY? FILL OUT THE REST OF THE
PAGE WITH AS MUCH INFO AS YOU CAN. DON'T SKIMP
ON THE DEETS! _____

_____

_____

_____

_____

_____

YOUR BFF IS THROWING A PARTY THAT SOUNDS A LITTLE CRAY-CRAY

Would you still go to her party if: (circle one)

ALL THE GUESTS HAVE TO WEAR SWIM FINS.   **YES** OR **NO**

SHE INVITES A PARTY CLOWN.   **YES** OR **NO**

THE PARTY IS BLUE CHEESE— THEMED.   **YES** OR **NO**

HER PET CHIPMUNK IS THE GUEST OF HONOR.   **YES** OR **NO**

HER PLAYLIST IS ONLY ACCORDION POLKAS.   **YES** OR **NO**

GUESTS CAN ONLY SPEAK IN RHYME.   **YES** OR **NO**

LEGENDARY!

Imagine you could invite anyone throughout all of history to a party. Would you get your groove on with Cleopatra? Or trade fashion tips with Queen Elizabeth I?

Pick Your *Top Five* Historical Invite List!

1. _____

2. _____

3. _____

4. _____

5. _____

Party-Vision!

Transform this ordinary room into the ultimate party palace. Add decorations, treats, games — maybe even a disco ball! Make this party yours.

Best Party EVER!!!

What was the most off-the-hook party you've ever been to?
What made it so awesome? Who was there? Was there a theme?
Write all about it here:

_____

_____

_____

_____

_____

_____

_____

_____

_____

_____

What kind of PARTY is Totes you?

For your party, what is the perfect outfit?

A. A T-shirt and your fave pair of jeans

B. Anything with sequins

C. A ball gown

Who's invited?

A. Your closest friends

B. Everyone who wants to come — and their friends, too!

C. Anyone with a nerdy side

What kind of music would you play?

A. Indie rock

B. Hip-hop

C. Classical music

What kind of food sounds good?

A. Popcorn

B. Chips and salsa

C. Petit fours

Results

PARTY
IS A:

Mostly A's:

MOVIE MARATHON—

Grab your BFFs and some snacks for a night of watching everyone's movie faves.

Mostly B's:

DANCE PARTY—

Crank up the music because your party is gonna be off the chain!

Mostly C's:

COSTUME BALL—

Put on your fanciest dress and get ready to party like it's 1899!

Party FORTUNE-TELLER

At your next slumber party, break out this fortune-teller and ask all your juiciest yes/no questions. Cut out the square below and use the directions on the next page to begin!

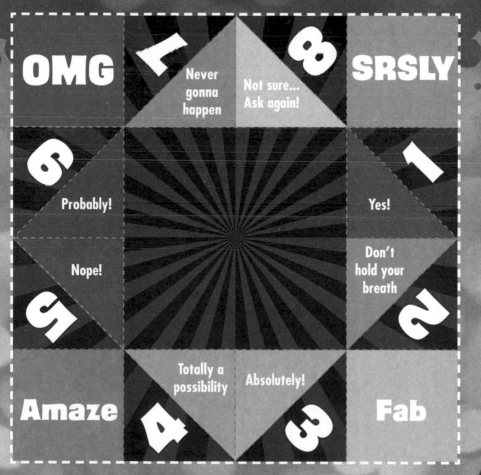

OMG

7

Never gonna happen

8

Not sure... Ask again!

SRSLY

6

Probably!

1

Yes!

Nope!

Don't hold your breath

5

2

Amaze

Totally a possibility

4

Absolutely!

3

Fab

Instructions:

1. With the text side facing down, fold all four corners into the center.

2. Flip the paper over and fold all four corners into the center again.

3. Fold the paper in half, then place your fingers inside each of the four corners.

4. Voila! Ask Away!

Dream Theme

Find out the perfect theme for your next party!

Which song is your main jam?

- ○ A. "Summertime" by Beyoncé
- ○ B. "All-American Girl" by Carrie Underwood
- ○ C. "Don't Stop Believin'" by Journey

Look through your closet. Which colors do you see the most?

- ○ A. Light blues and bold prints
- ○ B. Rich, earthy tones
- ○ C. Neon, neon, neon!

Which of these is so totally you:

- ○ A. Laid-back and relaxed
- ○ B. Always ready for an adventure
- ○ C. Dancing queen

Right now, your desktop background is:

- ○ A. A gorge beach somewhere warm
- ○ B. A galloping horse you wish you were riding
- ○ C. The vintage poster from your fave retro movie

Results

MOSTLY A'S:

Fly to the golden beaches of Hawaii for your luau-themed party! Whether you break out some limbo or start a hula contest, your guests will have an amaze time in the tiki-torch light.

MOSTLY B'S:

Get along to your rough-and-ready Western party. Guests can dust off their cowboy hats and boots for a rip-roaring good time. Yeehaw!

MOSTLY C'S:

Totally radical! Your 80s-themed party is gonna be gnarly to the max. Tease your hair as big as you can and grab your leg warmers to get ready for the party of the decade.

Everyone knows how to throw a good Christmas or Valentine's Day party. But what about some of the less well-known holidays? Show some **LOVE** for forgotten holidays with some *fab party ideas!*

RANDOM ACTS OF KINDNESS DAY

BAD POETRY DAY

TALK LIKE A PIRATE DAY

FEBRUARY 17TH:

AUGUST 18TH:

SEPTEMBER 19TH:

Take the Party with You

The party may be over, but you can give your guests a few party favors to remember the fun! Fill this gift bag with some awesome swag:

I'M SORRY, I CAN'T HEAR YOU OVER THE SOUND OF HOW AWESOME I AM!

Write some tweets telling the world about your next totes amaze vacay:

_____
_____
_____
_____
_____
_____
_____
_____**#BEACHBUM**

_____
_____
_____
_____
_____
_____
_____
_____
_____**#CITYLIGHTS**

_____
_____
_____
_____
_____**#ONTHEROADAGAIN**

Imagine you were given an unlimited budget to go on a different vacay with each one of your besties. Where would you go? Write about all the awesome stuff you'd get to see and do!

BFF#1's name _____ and I would visit _____

Because: _____

_____

_____

_____

BFF#2's name _____ and I would visit _____

Because: _____

_____

_____

_____

BFF#3's name _____ and I would visit _____

Because: _____

_____

_____

_____

RATHER EAT...

Cow tongue from France

OR

Fried tarantula from Cambodia?

Haggis from Scotland

OR

Bird's nest soup from China?

Cobra heart from Vietnam

OR

Pig's blood pancakes from Finland?

Bat soup from Micronesia

OR

Dried shark from Greenland?

Canned herring from Norway

OR

Tuna eyes from Japan?

WHERE SHOULD YOU GO FOR THE PERFECT VACAY?

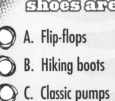

If you could have anything to eat right now, you'd have:

○ A. Mac and cheese
○ B. Something you've never tried before
○ C. Lemon-herb chicken breast with rice pilaf

Your fave pair of shoes are:

○ A. Flip-flops
○ B. Hiking boots
○ C. Classic pumps

On the weekend, you like to:

○ A. Chillax and read a book
○ B. Explore a new bike path
○ C. Visit museums

You'd love to spend an evening:

○ A. At a spa
○ B. Around a campfire
○ C. At a Broadway show

Results

MOSTLY A'S:

You're the queen of the beach scene! Head to the coast with your blanket and umbrella for your next totes chill vacay.

MOSTLY B'S:

Pack your bug spray, nature girl! You're ready for a camping adventure surrounded by some purple mountain majesty!

MOSTLY C'S:

It's the swanky city for your next vacay! With so many plays, museums, and galleries to see, don't forget to catch some ZZZs.

Travel Blues

HAVE YOU EVER BEEN ON A
TRIP WHERE ABSOLUTELY EVERYTHING
SEEMED TO GO WRONG? WHERE WERE YOU
TRAVELING? WHAT HAPPENED AND HOW
DID YOU DEAL WITH IT?
WRITE ALL ABOUT YOUR VACAY DISASTER HERE:

_____

_____

_____

_____

_____

_____

_____

_____

_____

IT'S A NOT-SO-

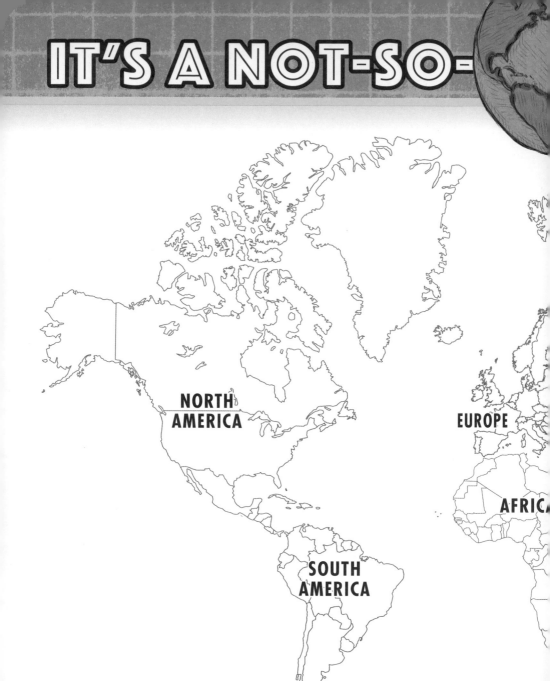

NORTH
AMERICA

EUROPE

AFRICA

SOUTH
AMERICA

Get your fave pen and color in all the countries you've visited.

SMALL WORLD!

ASIA

AUSTRALIA

Then choose a different color and fill in all the countries you'd like to visit!

Flip over to the map on the pages right before this one. Close your eyes, then point to a random place on the map.

WHERE DID YOUR FINGER LAND?

Write the 1st sentence of a story about you and your BFF visiting there. Then pass this book to her and have her write the next sentence. Keep going back and forth until your epic tale is finished!

_____

_____

_____

_____

_____

_____

_____

_____

_____

_____

_____

_____

What's your vacay personality?

First you need to choose a place to visit! You:

A. Go to the store and buy a ton of guidebooks

B. Check out your friends' vacay pics — they'll inspire you!

Now it's time to pack your bags. You:

A. Double-check your bag against the packing list you've been writing for weeks

B. Throw all your fave tops and skirts in first. Then look around the room for anything you missed.

During the flight to your destination, you:

A. Finish scheduling all your Must-Do Activities

B. Listen to music from the country you're going to visit

Oh, no! One of the museums you wanted to see is only open one day a week! You:

A. Frantically reorganize your schedule to make the new day work

B. Shrug. Maybe you'll check it out the next time you visit instead.

Results

VIA

MYVACAY

0021 V3 15041983

MOSTLY A's

You like to pack everything you can into your vacay. With your awesome schedule and a trusty guidebook, **NO SECOND OF YOUR TRAVEL ADVENTURE WILL GO TO WASTE!**

MOSTLY B's

Vacations are all about chilling out! Whether it's sitting by the pool or wandering through an art gallery, you like to live in the moment. **NO NEED TO SWEAT THE SMALL STUFF!**

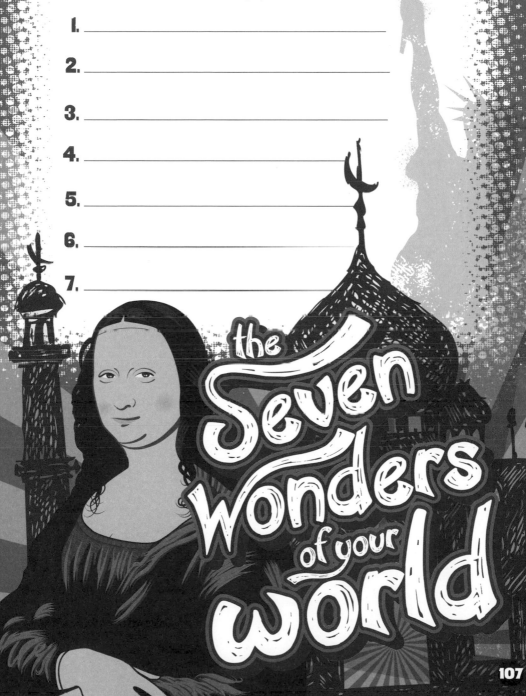

The Mona Lisa? The Statue of Liberty? **The Taj Mahal?**
List the Seven most wonderful things you'd love to travel to see:

1. _____

2. _____

3. _____

4. _____

5. _____

6. _____

7. _____

the Seven wonders of your world

PICTURE PERFECT

Draw the view from your ultimate vacay getaway and fill in the caption below!

Road Trip!

Plan a driving getaway for you and your besties!

You and your BFFs hop in the car and head to _____

On the way, you'll make sure to stop and visit _____

You might even visit a crazy tourist trap like _____

Make sure to pack snacks! What will you bring? _____

_____

Road trip playlist:

_____   _____   _____

_____   _____   _____

_____   _____   _____

To VACAY... AND BEYOND!

IMAGINE YOU COULD BE A TOURIST IN SPACE! WHERE WOULD YOU GO? WHAT WOULD SPACE TRAVEL BE LIKE? CHRONICLE YOUR FUTURE TRAVELS HERE:

COLOR THIS PAGE AND DRAW YOURSELF IN THE WINDOW:

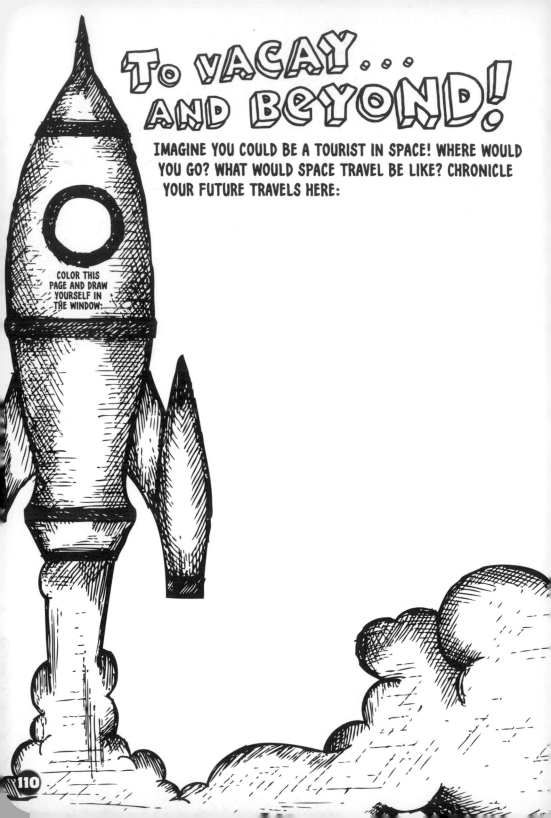

Do you have a Bucket List?

Write down all the amazing places and things you want to see someday. Then rank them in order from the sorta-wannas to the total-musts!

\#
_____

\#
_____

\#
_____

\#
_____

\#
_____

\#
_____

ROAD RULES

COLOR IN THE CITY USING YOUR FAVE COLORS AND CIRCLE YOUR ANSWERS BELOW.

True / False The driver gets to choose the music.

True / False Younger siblings have to sit in the backseat.

True / False Singing along with the radio is a must.

True / False Maps are for the weak.

True / False Trail mix is the best travel snack.

True / False The best vacay moments are spontaneous.